PRAISE F(

Death, With Occasion.

"The electrifying body of poems you find here in Tony Medina's *Death, With Occasional Smiling* speak with blood-soaked lips. The poet pulls us up from our knees, from the ashes of American history, imagination, and memory so that we can listen to the clarions of what we must all face if we are to ever be free. Facing language and self at once, Medina's intelligence, spirit, humor, and symphonic powers make language breathe in rhythms that resist bullets and blackface. Medina writes, 'Not enough lifetimes / To take back powder burn cries / To piece my boy back' as his readers are offered an orbit/obituary of the continued violence and systemic massacres of Black Lives. Tony Medina's poems speak our names in poems that cite blood, blues, and so much more as the Black Imagination persists in all its fury, triumph, grief, rage, bones, and joy. Medina, a poet whose voice has always been utterly original and innovative across crafts and forms, lashes and unleashes the truths of our ancestors and beyond to remind us all of our shadows, as well as the complicated textures, and tensions, of our flesh. These living poems are always-ever needed, as part of the threshing and reckoning we are burning down and rewriting in our time. The poet writes of this necessary justice in order to live and to love in America: 'I snatched the pistol / From the white man's / Mind.' The genius of Tony Medina requires us to breathe inside of our words and drums we are only really beginning to hear."

RACHEL ELIZA GRIFFITHS
author of *Seeing the Body* (W.W. Norton, 2020)

"Funk. Fly. F'real. Fresh. *Death, With Occasional Smiling* embodies the intellectual wanderings of William Carlos Williams, emotional genius of James Baldwin, and the wide gate of Pablo Neruda uncovering all things Bronx and Harlem under the sun by one of its favorite sons. It is cosmic in its signposting of a master poet, Tony Medina, a T.S. Elliot poet-technician of the unfolding American experience that is an America in an ongoing cultural war with itself. *Death, With Occasional Smiling* is the celebration with a twinkle in the eye or a wry smile. 'It is clear to see that Jesus was a conguero / Beating back bongo skins till his palms bled / Rorschach red.' A poet is a novelist jacked on the adrenaline rush that is the spirit populating the mind and animating the hand. 'Racism is an heirloom passed down through / Generations like a retrovirus / A rifle handed from father to son / Aiming to please some deep-seated heated / Urge to violate rape maim hurt some thing.' Bold pronouncements, sacrosanct revelations, simple truths are in the poet-shaman's bag of considerable magic-wisdom-funk. And Medina is a modern master. Medina understands that how a poet places a word on the page can disrupt the universe. Or a soul."

PATRICK A. HOWELL & TORI REID
co-founders of the storytelling company Victory & Noble

DEATH, WITH OCCASIONAL SMILING

DEATH, WITH OCCASIONAL SMILING

TONY MEDINA

POEMS

INDOLENT BOOKS

Published by Indolent Books,
an imprint of Indolent Arts Foundation, Inc.

www.indolentbooks.com
Brooklyn, New York
ISBN: 978-1-945023-26-2

Special thanks to Epic Sponsor Megan Chinburg
for helping to fund the production of this book.

For Tom Low—Gentleman, visionary
and pioneer of children's book publishing

In memory of Mari Evans, Ntozake Shange,
Hari Jones, Tiffany Austin, Naomi Long Madgett,
and Aldo Tambellini

CONTENTS

RUNNING THE VOODOO DOWN

You gotta have your tips on fire!

VICTOR HERNÁNDEZ CRUZ

DEATH, WITH OCCASIONAL SMILING

Arsonist Dies in Own Fire

I sat down on the couch
In the palm
Of the flame

That stretched its fingers
Out & up
To cup me

Like a man-eating
Tulip.
I sat there

Like I was watching
TV, concentrating on the
Cold sweet smell

Of gasoline, trying to keep
My mind off the
Sudden

Stench,
The black, choking,
Fatback smell
Of my burning flesh.

ONE GUY SHOT ANOTHER GUY

Dame un Traguito

It is clear to see that Jesus was a conguero
Beating back bongo skins till his palms bled
    Rorschach red

No need to put an accent over the e to know
Who he be—Claro que sí

Pah Pa Pah Pa   Cu Cu Cu-Roo

That he sang backup Boogaloo for Obàtálá
Swore by the hypnotic effects of a bolero

Caught in the throat of a rising sun suddenly
Sinking—a tecato's jones coming down

On 110th Street & Lexington Avenue
In the crusty eyelash of El Barrio

That he multiplied wine by sending his little cousin Pipo
To cop a few bottles from Pepo's bodega

Where he kept a Muscatel stash just beneath the
Alabaster statuette of San Lazaro &

Bustelo can urn of Doña Chicha's ashes
Atop the register with the faded Polaroids

Of his pregnant Tía in Ponce & his songless Tío
With the afro the size of Saturn in Sing Sing
Inked up from head to toe

It's plain to see that Jesus spoke in 4-4 time
& guaguancó

That he tapped his dusty rusty patent leather
Zapatos to a rhythm only the children
Of Africans & Indians understand

Bailando con Yemayá   Buscando la claridad

Singing: *El agua limpia todo*

O was he born in a manger or Morrisania Hospital
The critics will ask their silly questions like social
Workers dumb to the reality of the times
But Jesus will pay them no mind

Nor will he adhere to the census takers
Giving the side-eye to tax collectors

The only numbers he cares about come out
In New York or Brooklyn

So he could buy his baby a new pair of shoes
So he could walk on water—dried puddles of old wino piss

Or tap his toes trying to mimic the sound of dominoes
*Click*ing or ring fingers slapping against the stiff neck

Of beer bottles to once sun-baked viejitos in guayabera
Shirts & Panama hats, shouting—*¡MANTECA!*

Con cerveza breath working his arms & legs
Into a sweat-drenched rum-stench rumba
Furious frenzy as if despojando

Saying to no one & everyone in particular
What he begins to hear reverberating

Break dancing bomba planting
Plena in his inner ear—

　　　　¡Fíjate!

The Original

This is the thing, there actually was a time
I could leap tall buildings in a single bound.
Even with these bony ashy-ass knees. That was
Before Brylcreem and Afro Sheen
Slicked my Coif back like a swim cap—*Woo Cha*—

Had me hurtling through hot air and ghetto
Sky like a pissed-off seal on the steal. But then
All that Black Disobedient Civil Rights
Mimmy Jimmy hit the set and my black arse hit them
Power lines so quick was no time to hold

Back these damn unruly curls—they uncoiled
From this invisible-ass Ralph Ellison durag
Like bedsprings on a porno set—or some clumsy
Cop trigger itch. Mugs caught me hanging
Midair between lines, cables and string—

This here froage caught up between laundry
Drying like stretched and quartered scarecrows
From fire escape to fire escape—with no
Escape—as if this shit was an extended
Metaphor catch-22 for my dumb dangling

Dizzy black ass. The red boots and cape
Didn't help none. Motherfuckers still
Clowned my ass sun up sun down until

I finally hanged it all up and the white
Boy—once again—got the job. And the

Rest, as they say, is his story.

What Month Is Your History?

Your father collects scalps
    Your mother cries wolf through French Alps
Your father hangs flesh
    On Christmas trees
Your mother is puerile as the
    Driven snowplow—she's the bee's knees
Your father burns crosses

On front lawns to a crispy crunch
    Your mother packs lunch
Ham and cheese, an apple, milk
    Your father gives out blankets of smallpox silk
Your mother drapes flags
    Off porch banisters of bark
Your father paints welt marks

On a canvas of black skin, to a red paste
    Your mother is a pin-up doll advertising mace
Your father drops bombs of nuclear waste
    Your mother has good taste
Your father is decorated for his haste
    Your mother appreciates persimmons and scones
Your father tends a garden of bones

Diptych

In the Warehouse of Misery

War is a pornography of sorrow
Seldom denied

Kneecaps sunk in the dead
Black mouth of mud
Bones shaken out of skin

Skulls cracked like shells
A mother's wail ignored

Warehouse of moans

Limbs stockpiled sandbags
Buildings pocked & pulverized

Stamped out cigarettes
Smoke trailing from ashes
Ephemeral memory clouding

Toward a strange uncertain sky

The Gods Are Playing the Tambourines

The sky cracking like a whip
Roaring, roaring

Like a dog in heat, a cat on a hot tin roof.
There is a whisper in the rain.

A mist in the wind. A rumbling, grumbling growl.
Power surges through grilled, flame-broiled air.
Blackened catfish sky.
Is this the season of the witch, or
        Our summer of discontent?

Or is it just Mother Nature hiking up her dress and fanning,
Fanning herself something fierce from this unbearable heat
Showing us her teeth as she laughs furiously,
Furiously at our
                Irreducibility?

One Guy Shot Another Guy

One guy shot another guy, and so he went and got a gun. He came back and shot at the guy that shot at him, but hit another guy instead; and so he went and got a gun and came back shooting. A number of people heard gunshots and ran off to get some guns. This crossfire spread like wildfire until everybody had a gun. It got so bad they started shooting it out for bullets that were high on demand but low in supply. They couldn't make them soon enough until some started shooting the manufacturers for being slow on the draw. When all the bullets ran out, they started bashing each other over the head with the butts of their guns. There was so many pistol whippings and lumps and knots and busted heads and gun parts, people started belting one another with fists and poking each other's eyes out until everyone was blind with fury, tired as all hell, totally unarmed. The next day someone waited around like a stooge for his neighbor to fetch his mail in order to poke his eyes out.

O What a Time It Seems

O it was a panicky time
For pandemics, that is.
The lot of us could barely
Look at one another.
Such attitudes went viral;
No sooner could you clear
Your throat to speak
Before a gazillion eyes

Cut you down like grass.
A panicky time, indeed.
Those in charge of our
Every expression
Were expressionless.
Perplexed, they couldn't
Make neither heads or
Tails of this predicament

So we all rolled up our
Stares like yoga mats
And shut our doors
With a bang, never
To be seen again.
Funny, that was the
Second to last time
That sound was ever heard

Before grass and flowers
And bees and blue jays

Sprang up around
Two naked beings
Giggling in a garden,
One to another,
And the other laughing
Lightheartedly at a leaf.

Mythology for Beginners

Three wise men brought me
Gifts: handcuffs, a white jacket &
A gurney to roll me to the back of a
Padded patty wagon, with nice bright
Red & white lights cutting through
The dark. Are you gonna eat that spare rib?
Does ice skating constitute walking
On water? I too wanted to bash my
Brother's head in with a rock,
The motherfucker always got the
Biggest piece of chicken—& I'm
The oldest! I wouldn't let a shorn
Woman near me with a pair of
Salad tongs, let alone scissors. I'd
Climb a mountain or two to drop
Some tabs. Shit, I'd have a conversation
With some burning bush, and chant to
Gods, chant to gods. I walked by a
Slingshot, talking about the Bloods or
Crips. I was blind & now I see.
I too rose from the dead, with a little
Help from Viagra & a McDonald's
Hand puppet. Her thong was a red sea I
Parted with my lips & tongue. It was
Liberating. She said, *Ahh-oh, let my
Pubics go!*

Aiming to Please

We've always wanted flame-broiled walls
Peppered by mortar rounds. We've always
Longed for glass in the wind, mustard gas
On dry skin, pale porous malnourished shins.
We have so much time to waste; our bodies
Sacrificed in haste, hurling makeshift explosives
Molotov cocktails at tanks and walls in-

Different as rich men with bad taste. Isn't
It aesthetically *pleasing* to paint a
Blue sky black, to blot out the sun, to in-
Cinerate the earth? We love to enter-
Tain you, to amuse you, to make you grin
And laugh your head off with our cries and in-
Cessant wailing. Oh to be born into

This explosive fanfare endless shell shock
Parade of silent screams. How shall we pre-
Sent our skulls? How meticulous shall
We lay out our bones in the museum
Display case of your selective memory?
In what grave shall our history be buried?

Father, Son Arrested in the Death of . . .

Racism is an heirloom passed down through
Generations like a retrovirus

A rifle handed from father to son
Aiming to please some deep-seated heated

Urge to violate rape maim hurt some *thing*
Not unlike your teen friend whose dad fingered

Some pre-cooked red meat
But that father-son bond over dead things

The deer caught in your sight blindly
Enjoying the green grass and the breeze

Before the shot rings out like a cracked whip
Brown buck buckling like the felled jogger

Fighting for each breath clutching at what poured
From his black body staring at white teeth

Brother, Can You Spare a Crime?

A bullet meant for a stye in the eye
A bullet for each cry-caught throat—
Cricket cracking in tall grass
A bullet for laughter rolling off
Wind stirred by an empty far-off swing
A bullet for the wino at the corner
Bonfire who sings to the flapping tongue

Of flames coughing in patches of cold
A bullet for the soul & heart & bone of passersby
Going about their business mindless
A bullet to undress anger shake
Down rage force frustration to
Pay the piper of the pauper lost
In a labyrinth & daze

A bullet for the haze the foggy
Debris of memory that once
Valued blood pumping in the
River of human veins
A bullet for the brain that strains to
Understand the incomprehensible
The senseless slaughter of smoke

Caught in the curbside tug-o-war
Of gravity & depravity
A bullet for each pulse of heart

Beating out a purple Plena
In the land of plenty that has *nada*
Nada y pues nada but bullets
To spare

Senryu for Trayvon Martin

Skittles bag singe–
Stippled holey
Bleeds in rain puddle

Hoodie hides
No blood, tears, or
Eyes shut by wet grass

Screams pierce night sky
A father's stomach pits
My boy! My boy!

Shot through sky
Skittles like Roman candle bursts
Blood from open chest

Stars squint and stare
Raindrops glare in moonlight
Witnessing bloodletting

Mourning grass
Like wet face of boy
Screaming bloody murder

Gunpowder blinds
The eye of justice reckless
As a dumb vigilante

Silence of blood clouds

Night drizzle where wind
Whistles through hole in can

Empty bag of Skittles
Crushed can of iced tea
Last game with father

Rain chews night air
Gnaws at brown boy flesh
Grinning teeth of bullets

Rain stains brown boy's
Back as blood pours from chest
Turning the green grass red

How Blues Is Born

Rain falls steady on dead end
Street strewn with black body

Mama's cries hang
On rain hooks ornamenting
Night wind's grin

Blood petals pock
Grim face of grass like lotus
On rain slick back of black boy

Not enough lifetimes
To take back powder burn cries

To piece my boy back

Bert Williams

The only thing I wanted
From shoe polish was

        The shine—

What you look for:
        Reflection

Covered up in
A mask of

        Black slime

Under the stage light glare:
The familiar stare,

The private mirror
Scare,

Weary &
        Aware—

Looking back,

        Haunting me

Banner Day

I had a stunt double that played Othello in blackface.
Crypto Stay Puft Marshmallow mofo said, *I wanted to be*
Black a more. Had a poster of Bert Williams in his trailer.
I knew the signature wasn't his by the way he neglected
To dot the I's and cross the T. Bert didn't do that shit.
He'd come to the set whistling Dixie, then turn sideways
On his makeup chair singing, *You can call me Al* . . .

Capping that off with an off-the-cuff—*Mammy!*
As if he just took a swig of Coke or snorted the shit.
One time he bragged about doing Repertory Theater
In the Chi playing a broke-down Hamlet. *I really wanted*
To play Macbeth, but the whole play was a bloody mess,
He said. One day he came to the set tore the fuck
Up. His breath could burn your brow. I could hardly

Decipher the script at the table reading. Rolled up
To me and said, *What makes you so special? I'm the one*
Doing the heavy lifting, taking all the hits and falls. I cut
My eyes to him bearing down deep into his blue-eyed soul.
Said, *Don't let this light skin fool you. That fucked up*
Weave and Bert Williams doesn't give you a pass, mane.
Give you that one-drop molly-whop—ya feel me?

I will still open a can of green whoop-ass on you
Sure as you're standing in the shadow of my piss
With that slushy in your hand smelling like Cutty Sark

And yeasty Wonder Bread sweat, Opie. Then some cat
From Costume carted him away like Blanche DuBois and
Sprayed his big ass down with green paint, dressing him in
A lobster bib and tore up terrible twos toddler trousers.

Charleena Lyles

O, I see—you want me to believe
I gave birth to this moment instead of those three children
Not fully woke cowering behind this cracked door

You want me to believe that this moment will blossom
Like my will to have another

But this possibility that stretches my belly
Protected by the shadow of the blade trembling
In dim hallway light at the military presence

Of police leaning against my door against the battering ram
Knock quaking the floor hammering about inside my
Head—you want me to believe that the intruder I called you for
Is me—That these children whose black flesh I protect
With my very life are at risk—in danger—not from those bullets
You dislodge into my 78-pound flesh into my stomach and chest
To stunt the blooming growth of black life in my black body

But me

That I am the wolf at my own door and this blood splattered
Across white hall walls and splintered sunlight
Pagan ritual against my very breath—my audacious breathing

From the Crushed Voice Box of Freddie Gray

I am the Magic Negro
The Black Houdini
Who done it
Done it to him self

I handcuffed my own
Damn self
I threw myself
In the back of the patrol car

My hands shackled
Behind my back
Slaveship cargo
Ago

I am the Magic Negro
The Black Houdini
Who done it
Dooze it to him
Self him black self

See, Ma? No hands!

I snatched the pistol
From the white man's
Mind
From the back of the
Patrol car—

Suck on dis, Houdini!
I grabs the gun
And shoot my
Self in the chest
Neo-colonial style

The autopsy report says
Damn—
Would've been easier
To walk on water
I bet you a quarter
He done shot himself

I am the Magic Negro—
Spineless—

I brokes my own spine
After hogtying myself
Into a pretzel even
Houdini who done it
Would envy

Only to turn myself
Into a human pinball
Rattling around
The steel gullet
Of a Negro pickup truck

Once reserved for newly-
Arrived Potato Famine
New York Irish drunks
Down on their luck—

Me—*moi*—
It is I who was
Othello—
Oh hell no—

Yes—me
The Magic Negro
The Black Houdini
Who done it—
Dooze it all the time

To him self
His own
Damned self

#IfIDieinPoliceCustody

If I die in police custody
Know that I am not Houdini
That hole in my chest
Did not magically appear

Regardless of my hands
Cuffed behind my back
That I preferred my blood
Inside my body instead
Of pouring through

Powder-burned flesh
Pooling at my feet
In the backseat
Of some patrol car

If I die in police custody
Don't let my bone fragments
Puzzle the public
When the police insist
I reached for a gun

That if I had magic powers
I would not use them
To end my little life
But to save it

A Few Small Nips

They dragged the girl in
　　From the frontline
　　　　　　Blood was everywhere
　　Even the framed crow of death above
The mattress drank her blood

And tried to eat
　　Her broken body
But no matter
　　The number of wounds
　　　　Or the amount of blood

　　　　　　Lost, she still insisted
On getting her other shoe
　　And naked—and without arms—
　　　　Ran out into the face of her fate
　　Like an open pomegranate

The Broken Column

My body stiffens at
The muscle and pores.
Each morning, sunlight
Creeps through the pane
Shrouds me in a hot
Metal shawl, my spine
A shattered column

Of stone, splitting
My torso in two.
I stretch to breathe
New life into my blood
And bones.
But from each pore

A nail springs,
Replacing the most
Invisible of hairs.
Each hole resurrects
A tombstone, marking
My dreadful crawl
To the grave.

In the Window of the Cuchifrito Joint

The idea of ancestry: Mixed blood,
Plunder the wonder of gold foretold:
Slit noses, scalps counted,
What white men stood for:

Manifest Destiny. Bibles hold
A controlling interest in the mind
Of the uncivilized whose gods betrayed,
Whose myths led them astray shackled in mines

Fast forward centuries: Bloodline displayed
Behind Plexiglas frozen history:
A language like no other: Clinical
Calculation no bloody mystery

Enough to make optimists cynical:
Time's divided by lustful bayoneting,
History's a hanging pig's bloodletting

I Carry My Father's Name in My Name

He is a shadow I bury just the same.
His face, pitch as an African night,
Is my face, yet I can't remember *it*.

He comes to life to me through tales
Mama tells: How they met in college
On an island far from their homes;
He and she galaxies apart

Made an unlikely pair of planets orbited
By stares and glares when they held hands,
Their ebony-ivory fingers laced like striped ribbons.
But we did not care, Mama says, showing

Me his photo, the one where he has glasses,
A pipe—and a great big grin—my grin.
She reminds me love is *colorblind.*
I must be too, I think, seeing my father's face

In a photograph, as if for the first time.
I never noticed that he did not look
Like Mama or my sister Mary or Gramps and Toots.
His face is like my face, his smile, *my* smile.

Yet, I deny him when friends come by,
Asking, *Who's the black man in the photographs?*
Or at parent-teacher nights when everyone's dad
Shows up, and I pretend I don't have one.

Sammy

With 60 lbs barely stitching my flesh
To brittle bone gristle and gray tones
How much of that 60 you think
My glass eye weighed in my wife's

Hand stripping me of what jewelry was
Left as I succumbed to cardiac arrest the
Cancer in my throat belting out its last song
Vibrating through cocktail napkin bones

Folded ash smoke soul slipping out
Its tray laying there hard and stiff
Like cicada shells, *What kind of fool*
What kind of fool am I, I ask my wife in song

As she rolls my dead body over like a seat
Cushion hiding change

CITY OF
FLOATING COFFINS

City of Floating Coffins

It was a tiny city, or seemed tiny, because everyone carried a coffin. The streets were flooded with people traveling in fours, sometimes even sixths, lugging around dead people (loved ones, even) in wooden boxes, who had collapsed like tipped cows from some disease or heartache or setback, or failure. And this sudden collapse from breathing and eating, and shitting and fucking, and lying and scratching, and cheating and stealing, would even threaten to set the steady monotonous procession of citizens (condemned to pall bearing) should one become instantly overcome with severe weight loss of one's every ounce and pound. Some didn't care and spent the better part of their afternoons saying it was God trying to teach them a lesson about being selfish and greedy and illiterate and lazy and promiscuous, indulging in too much food and drink, trinkets and TV, microwaves, computers, automobiles, shoes, clothes and almost anything made of plastic and steel from cheap and foreign labor, wiping out trees, covering every inch of earth with the dull gray slabs of rough concrete or the hot smooth black of tar, blotting out the sky and sun and moon and stars with black noxious soot. But now almost everyone in the fast city was dressed in black. And the city was not so fast. People crept along the avenue, sweating beneath hats hammered onto their swollen skulls by the sun's persistent rays, straining from the weight of a loved one. The thing is, no one dared to get out of line, spring a quick step off the curb to hail a cab. Morgues were empty. Funeral parlors were empty, too. All subsequently went out of business. But it wasn't a total loss for capital: Coffin manufacturers fought tooth and nail to find trees to make more coffins—which were definitely in great demand—and the workers (who were dropping like flies) to employ their labor and chop the trees and shape them into pretty boxes to carry ugly people.

They winced at the thought of having to resort to using prison labor to make their coffins. The streets are not safe enough as it is with these bloody plagues, let alone an army of thugs running around loose with chainsaws and axes, came the cry from the city council; until one of their scientists came up with the idea of making plastic coffins. Though it seemed like a good idea, detractors complained that the streets would look like an endless Tupperware party with human corpses basting like pigs on a spit or chickens in a window display case on a rotisserie. But more people dropped like flies. Apparently, they believed in science but not dialectics. After all, social scientists argued, think of how lovely it would be to be able to always see your loved ones—kind of like a viewing that never ends, until you do. Your loved ones would always be in view and on display as if they were still with us—not locked away in some dark, dank wooden box with its lid clamped shut forever to roam the streets of Purgatory. This is the argument that sold them on the plastic see-through coffins. In another city, half a century ago, the entire population was nearly cremated by a bomb. It was rumored, by citizens of nearby cities and towns, survivors dressed their loved ones in T-shirts that asked: *Will You Keep Me When I'm Gone?* The survivors themselves wore shirts that said: *You Bet!* But in this tiny city of floating coffins flooding the narrow streets like yellow cabs clogging the arteries of its midtown and downtown shopping areas, the survivors practiced this ritual not in words but deeds. To be kept meant literally kept: lugged around in a coffin box from sun up to sun down and kingdom come, or come what may.

Antwon Rose

Roses are supposed to be red not bleed red. Teenagers are supposed to graduate from high school go on to college live out our dreams not collapse on black asphalt from three bullets in the back by a trigger-happy cop, hating-fearing black boys. Roses are red and I am no longer living I'm dead for being black and boy for being black and out-and-about for being black at the wrong place at the wrong time for being black and breathing for being black and fearing no matter what the cop pulled me over for I was as good as dead. So I did what many would've done run but not faster than the rapid fire of a gun trained to do just that shoot black boys in the back I could not out run the three bullets that stabbed through my thin 17-year-old back one after the other after the other eating through flesh and bone coughing up blood red and wide and thick as petals. Roses are supposed to be red not bleed red. Teenagers are supposed to be living and breathing laughing and dreaming and messing around we're supposed to be hugging our moms and dads our aunties and uncles at graduation. I should be alive and breathing enjoying my blackness and being.

Diptych

Still Life

Trees freeze their arms missing their leaves
Snowflakes hang from branches and choke

    Homeless man without a coat
    Street grater crucifix of smoke

Still Life

Screams scattered in wind
    A child crawls to her father
        His cracked skull a brown soup bowl

Ode to Bodega Cats

They lay around like that one chancla
You could never find, then spring up
From nowhere, narrowly knocking
Down that last box of pigeon peas
And rice left over from the Nixon
Administration with layers of dust
Thick enough to trampoline off.

They help you pick the wrong
Winning Lotto numbers,
Scratching a random claw drawn
And retracted from an unseen paw
As you scrutinize the card in the dim
Bodega light having forgot your
Reading glasses, once again.

When you take 8 years to decide
Whether you want a Ring Ding
Or a slice of pound cake wrapped
In what resembles the sofa slip-
Covers your grandmother bought
Just before summer to have the
Seat cushions glue themselves

To the back of your thighs
Right before you head out the door
To hang out with your friends when
She says, *Mi'jo, bring me back*
A Devil Dog and a Pepsi—

And don't forget to bring me back
My change!

It is the bodega cat who puts
You on blast, meowing into
The store PA system asking
Aloud if there's any more
Kotex or Goya beans in
Aisles 3 and 4 so that everyone
On your block could clown

You for the rest of your life.
No, you can't kill a bodega cat.
Those mofo's will cut you
With a quickness, their claws
Swifter than a Swiss Army or
Ginsu knife, blunter than a ball-
Peen hammer or those Phillies

You get in lieu of Bambú
Paper the bodega cat
Shreds sharpening his claws
Just to fuck with you as he
Lays back smoking a well-
Rolled joint along the dusty
Cans of motor oil no one

Buys because they don't
Have rides—*This is the 'hood,*
My mellow! Where bodega
Cats don't fucks with mice
And ride the backs of rats like

Bronco bulls rambling through
The projects like Pamplona.

Bodega cats are badass bitches,
Ghetto snitches, they scratch
That ass before it itches, leap
Up on counters that smell like
Fishes. They like Bébé's kids—*They*
Don't die, they multiply—and will swat
And swipe a motherfucker like a fly!

They will leave some stank piss
For you and have your Häagen-Dazs
Pint grow hair. Hell, you may
Spot one with a mouse tail dangling
From its slant smile like a gold-tooth
Cheshire or uptown Mona Lisa stuck
On a porcelain throne having run out

Of toilet paper.

Ay! Ay! Ay! Ay!

1. He worked for Horatio Hal's House of Cars.

2. In his first three months he sold a hubcap and
   What was left of a glove compartment.

3. His family nearly starved on what he made on commission.

4. He had to pawn his gold-tooth smile in order to stretch
   the soup.

5. Knocking off bodegas in Harlem never crossed his mind. Be-
   sides,
   The musty basement smells and old, black chewing gum embedded
   In the dirty tiles turned his stomach every time he went in for a
   Budweiser, Lay's potato chips, and Now and Laters.

6. Sometimes he referred to his mother as Mom Dukes.

7. This could've had something to do with the fact that she was a
   Corrections officer at Rikers.

8. This, before the days when she used to run numbers on
   Simpson Street
   In the South Bronx and was in a gang called The Disciples, totin' a
   Machine gun, as Prince once put it.

Coitus Interruptus

9. Mom Dukes on growing up:

"I wanted to be a lesbian.
But, of course, Mama wasn't hearing it.
She thought I wanted to be a thespian.
It took me ten years to get out of acting school!"

10. He left Horatio Hal's for a one-man mariachi band.
    You could find him on a corner any given Sunday,
    Harassing tourists and passersby, keeping the homeless
    Up all night with his constant—

Ay, ay, ay, ay
Canta no llores!

Inline Skating

They were ordinary people
Regular folks, as they used to
Say back in the day,
Who worked dead-end,
9-to-5, taxpaying jobs
Monday through Friday
Sun up, sun down

Who got smashed on Saturday
Went to church on Sunday
Got used to the phrase—
Attention, Kmart shoppers!
Till Walmart pushed them
Away, sent them hurling
To the Unemployment Parade

They were ordinary people
Who spoke in simple sentences
With few adverbs and staunch
Conservative metaphors
In Christian cloths
Even though their paychecks
Crumble like moths

They were ordinary people
Who read their bibles
And waved their flags

Whose color they could cash
In on depending upon the
Direction of the wind
And if skin was still a sin

Two Eintou: Stevedore, Louisiana

Cotton
Bale on my back
Life's all work & welt marks
I drag these bones across the plains
Working for someone else
Days are long &
Rotten

Rotted days
Are long & working
For someone else's a drag
Like these bones lugged across these plains
All work & life's welt marks
On my bale-back
Cotton

Bones in Tow

Faces gathered
In stone

Survive
Centuries of rain

This ocean that
Swallows

Holds bones
In tow

A broad
Wet

Back
Many have crossed

Chain rust
Red raw link

Welted marks
What is carried

Inside
Each raised

Ridge
Cries of ancestors

Faces gathered
In stone

Oscar Peterson

Piano rainfall
    Jelly roll

Ebony fingers on
    Ivory box

Maharajah of the Keyboard
    Wasn't a chord

You couldn't strike
    Quick and precise as

Lightning
    Each note a string

Each key a ring
    In the heart

Instant composer
    Of the intellectual art

Where have you gone
    Where will you go

Taking back your blues
    Solo

Poem for Hugo Chávez

Because you know
That pain is not
Our motherland

That suffering
Is not our
Divine right

That heaven is
What we make
On earth

Like houses
Love
And bread

Because you come
From the heart
Of the soil

And do not sprinkle us
With holy water
Pie-in-the-sky lies and
Ashes to ashes dust to dust

Because you know
That your big mouth
And your curly hair

Is African
And your brown skin
And dark eyes is Indian

Because you don't point
To Europe for
Beauty or salvation

Because you know
As Che and Fidel and
Maurice Bishop and Roque Dalton

And Walter Rodney
And Neruda and Allende
And Patrice Lumumba

That life is what
We make with our
Hands

Because you know as Jesus
That it is not difficult to
Multiply bread and fish

That oil is not
The lifeblood
Of the earth

That it should not
Run through our veins
Like fear

Because you are David
In the shadow
Of Goliath

And know that
The price of freedom
Is love

Still Life with Rick James Braids, Red Dream Book and Velvet Jesus

I'm a leaning tower of 8-track tapes,
Dust-sparkled in the living room sun,
Gleaming against burnt coffee table
Ash before an altar of plastic slipcovers,
A 72-inch of James Brown singles—*Say it*
Loud, I'm black and I'm proud—*Baby-*
Baby-baby baby-bay-beh screams crackling
Static into the air, ricocheting off
      Crystal bead curtains dangling like
      Rick James braids in the doorway, a
      Runner rolled out like a dog's tongue
      To protect the brand spanking new
      Carpet my aunt's number hitting
      In Brooklyn paid for, her red dream
      Book underlined and circled with
      Black eyeliner and blue Bic pen.
No one has any use for the coasters
Or album covers used by tattooed
Uncles for sifting weed and coke
And hanging on walls like Black
Velvet Jesus poker game art above
The dull shine of linoleum worn
Down and scuffed by Pumas and Pro-
Keds and Salsa pumps' hustle twirls.

Sunday Morning So Soon

Can I enter as rain on the slick back
Of wind bent between each kiss like waves?
I want to wade through the tender part of you,
Glide along smooth skin, part you like

An ordained sea, red and raw as flames.
When you are wet with curiosity,
When raindrops find no end in the labyrinth
Of what you remember, when wind cries,

Dried only by the faint stare of words
On the page from the book you devour,
When touch is natural as breathing
And each breath forsakes the wall you have

Erected to protect your heart from the
Possibility of rain seduced from
Storm cloud, that sound you hear, that
Constant tapping, me leaning into you.

Two Days after Christmas

Her whole life, every choice she's ever made,
Has led her to this moment, a little
Before 9 in the morning, two days after
Christmas, a chill stabbing through her flesh and
Bone, her two-year-old screaming hysterically,
His hands around her neck. Clumping dirty
Snow still crushed up against the curb, outside

Her window, leaning into a slant of
Sun, a whole week and a half after the last
Snowfall. His hands carried that cold like a
Shawl—or a second skin clinging weed smells
And some thot's pussy smell, yet that little
Whiff wouldn't last a minute before her
Eyes bulged white to red to brown in less than

A few seconds, she couldn't even gasp
For air, her daughter's screaming plea of—
Mami Mami Mami faintly ringing
And whispering in the cold dry air—*Ma-*
Mi Mami Mami—Her foot shifted—but
There was no stair, only the screaming, the
Cursing, the Facebook Live selfies, the down-

On-one-knee, the wedding ring in a white
Pork fried rice box, the pleas the pleas the *please*
Baby please I'll never do you wrong again pleas,

Only the toddler's crying, the snow outside,
The remembering to do laundry,
The electric bill, the call to her sister
To call 911, he's acting crazy again.

Sometimes I'm Happy

Coffin box of words
No sun penetrates this day
Rain along my back

I want to hold you
Flowers turn to ash in hands
Blow away like dust

Something is crumbling
Inside smoke swirls from ashtray
Twisted halo grief

Climbs up inside me
Sits and stays awhile stirring
Me like a stiff drink

I want to sink not
Swim in the ocean of you
Swish and swirl and sing

Bluely this gray noon
Spread across a mustard sky
Missing you too soon

Moment's Notice

Coltrane, a coal train
A cold rain of diamonds
Washing over me
Soft and wet as tulips
Misty in the morning sun

I want a bouquet of sighs
My lips on your thighs, no lie
I want your eyes spying
The trace of my fingertips
Contemplating the taste of your lips

Can I slip the honey dip
Caress and coo that part of you
That purrs, that stirs—
Last night I dreamt we shared
A raincoat in the pouring rain

Your earlobe in my mouth
You danced in puddles
Like a little girl in a pink raincoat
Last night I dreamt we eloped
Down a slippery slope

Like Alice in Wonderland
Pan's Labyrinth
We turned our love into
A fairytale buried in some old book
Fallen from the shelf

Last night I dreamt we were
A pile of clothes slumped
On the bathroom floor
The cold tile pressed against
Your back, me raining on you

An endless trickle of lips
I have fallen like a leaf
Kissing your tender toes
Who knows what love will bring
I want to celebrate the fact

That in your eyes there's spring
Sunset sprinkling through clouds
Sky an ice cream canvas
Rollercoaster ride in your eyes
My feet barely touching ground

When you're around

Deep Sea Blues

I kept walking toward the sea
    Until I couldn't see
Said I kept walking into the sea
    Until I couldn't see

The sea must've put a spell on me
    Cause it lulled me
In its arms
    Like I was its baby

Said the sea put a spell on me
    Rocking me
In its arms
    As if it was kin to me

Now don't get me wrong
    I wasn't thirsty, hot, or in need of a bath
Said I wasn't thirsty, I wasn't hot
    Or in need of a saltwater bath

I carried my heart in a bucket
    And my tears in a flask
Said I carried my heart in a bucket
    And my tears in a Muscatel flask

The day I barged in the boss' office
    Demanding he give me a raise
The time I walked in my boss' office
    Asking him to up my pay

Only to find my wife on his lap
   And they with nothing to say
Said I found my old lady on his desk
   And they didn't stop to say

A damn thing before I went postal
   And blew them both away
Said I capped off a few buckshots
   And sent their blood a-spray

Then headed out to the sea
   To wash their blood away
I headed out to the deep blue sea
   Washing away that memory

Double Dare

Was the cop kneeling on George Floyd's neck
As he lay gasping for his last breath praying
To his white Jesus was he taking a
Knee to shine a light on police brutality
Was he brutal when he rocked back and forth
Like a hobby horse applying pressure
Did the rocking make him think about his
Childhood was he daydreaming with one
Hand in his pocket cowboy ritual applying
More and more pressure as George Floyd managed
To cry out for his dead mother *I can't breathe please*
Your knee is on my neck I can't breathe I can't breathe
Was he caught up in his childhood days
Magically thinking he was back on that

Dime store horse or on top of his Amy
Cooper or Karen or any old Becky bronco
Breaking from his past aggressively groping
Applying all that pressure as pedestrians
Pleaded with him to stop to stop to stop
Did the cop get his rocks off as he rocked
Back and forth until George Floyd was no longer
Pleading did he enjoy taunting George Floyd's
Limp flesh as a piss stream leaked out of his black
Body along with his last breath when the
Lynch mob photo-op gleam in his eyes
Whispered to a dead George Floyd *Get up*

Get up Get up as if a dare a double
Dare or a simple dime store memory

    Giddy up Giddy up Giddy up

Holy Communion

My mother turns me into a sponge
Pockmarked with cigarette burns

My skin's grim red lips
Pursed through melt of brown

She wants to burn the devil
Out of me, each hot wet

Mark brings me closer to
The Holy Ghost, every ash & singe

Makes me scream
For my lord Jesus

Under my bed or in back
Of the closet, my heart

Clangs into my chest
A question rings & rings

Inside my head
Is it a sin is it a sin

To love the smell of burning skin
More than God or kin

Broke Campaign Contribution

When I announced
I was running
For Mayor
Of a Dark Alley
All I got
Was piss

And the occasional side-
Eye from a rat
Sucking his teeth
Whining about
Me fucking up
His high

Broke Lives Matter

I got that new job standing on the
Corner talking shit and drinking 40s
Had to audition for it.
Took me all damn day
To drink all them 40s
Afterwards, I didn't have shit
To say except if you see my kidneys

Floating along the curb
In a steady stream of piss dreaming
Of sailing to Byzantium
Don't step into them like galoshes
Stomping through puddles
Like a three-year-old *enfant terrible*
Blow them up like Luft balloons

And send them back my way
I could dry them out on this here
Concrete street
Use them as sponges
Pray they don't smell like fungus
Juggling them with my feets
For quarters

Song Without a Flag

I am undocumented
I have no docks to lament

My tears make sea levels rise
High water marks on my chin

This is my disguise
I move by moonlight

Stars map out my flight
At daybreak I wade through

Water, sift through sand
That choir you hear

The wind at my back
Somehow whistling *Dixie*

Through my rib
Cage

If You Spill an Horchata

If you spill an horchata
On your purple Barney romper
Because somebody crashed
Into your trailer-park
Camper that crumpled up
Like dirty clothes in a hamper,
Chances are your life's gonna
Get damper. And if your
Anger just so happens
To cause small opportunistic
Mammals to scamper
Away from your horchata hostility
Crushed beer-can camper
And a scurry of squirrels:
Irate, angry, and otherwise,
Kick a Radio City Music Hall
Cancan on the front lawn of your
Animated animosity with such
Velocity you attempt to join in
Turning your bum hip into a
Slinky, so much so when you turn
Right, it hangs a left
And the fire department
Can't seem to fetch it from
The old oak tree and you pray
The fat firefighter doesn't get
Stung by a bee—and you end
Up like Kaepernick taking a knee be-
Cause standing awkwardly on one leg

Sends the flames of hell's fury
Running up your spine like
Vengeful gasoline, chances are
Your life is gonna be hampered.

Carrying Candelabras, Quoting Oscar Wilde

Did Walter Mercado predict
The return of the cicadas?
The ones with pompadours
Streaked in silvery gray strands
And gold sparkling specks?

The ones that carry candelabras
And quote Oscar Wilde, wishing
To hang around like Dorian Gray,
Framing arguments about their

Jealousy and hatred of coquis
Whose sound is closer to Salsa
Than their broken maraca screams?
Are we to accept such *Cha Cha-Cha Cha-Cha Cha*

Cha Cha-Cha Cha-Cha Cha? Or will we resist
The cataclysmic cyclone of cloned
Castanets creeping and crawling
Along our crooked chakras? Should
Compassion be contagious? Or are we

Just wasting our time, clumsily crushing
It beneath beer-canned feet like cicadas
Sounding like hard shell tacos masticating
In our mouths, between the glint and glee

Of gleamingly indifferent teeth, smiling like
Liberace, staring at the camera, cooing—
I wish my brother George was here?
Did Walter Mercado predict the coming
Of the cicadas—or am I just bugging?

RUNNING
THE VOODOO DOWN

Partial Transcript of Richie Incognegro's Fox Interview

"I may be pasty. I may be hasty. I may be a waste of a good egg &
skeet. I may be inked up with Hepatitis B and annoyingly bombastic,
spastic, boorish & whorish. I may be a gross exaggeration of obesity.
I may be an obsequious brute to my own caveman-dwelling genetic
li(n)e. I may have arteries the size of blood sausages stuffed with the
ass-end of a pig roasting on a spit in the window display case of a
condemned Hooters closed down for forcing the roasted pig to wear
fishnet stockings. I may be functionally illiterate & sleep with barn-
yard animals. I may be a boring inane drone whose idea of a good
time is whacking off to war films. I may scratch my ass in public and
take an axe handle to jock itch. I may be a sexist Neanderthal with
the breath of Vikings enthralled with being the biggest asshole this
side of Rush Limbaugh's crystal meth acne-riddled Porky the Pig
ass. I may have hairy man-a-teats that'll give you the side-eye in
the shower. I may be white. I may be trashy. I may be bloated, red &
rashy. My drawers may be mashy. I may down three kegs of beer for
breakfast then pass gas in a crowded elevator. I may be the dumbest
fatheaded meat eater this side of a wet squat thrust. I may even wear
Ku Klux Klan drawers & enjoy a cross burning or two. I may even
think I'm an honorary black man because I've listened to a few rap
songs, can hurl around the N-word like it's a one-way boomerang
causing a clang. And I may assault black women with golf clubs
thinking I'm entitled to hump on whomever I damn well please with
the divine right of Thomas Jefferson & my other founding fathers.
I may give interviews on FOX news, wear the Confederate flag like
Depends. Heck, I may even vote Tea Party or Republican, if I knew
what voting was. I may even gargle & rinse with racial epithets
& have sex with sheep in blackface while Al Jolson moans in the

background to D.W. Griffith jacking off on the silver screen mean mugging slaves—but I am no racist. Ask my teammates. All them niggers know that. I swear on my mother's testicles."

Sunken Place Blues

You can't get coffee
You can't ask for directions
You can't carry a cellphone
You can't go to your backyard
You can't sit on your front porch
You can't stand on the corner
You can't sit in your car
You can't purchase a BB gun
You can't carry a legally registered gun
You can't walk the street
You can't wear a hoodie
You can't reach for your wallet
You can't have your hand in your pocket
You can't hold your hands in the air
You can't run away
You can't play your music
You can't smile or stare
You can't move a muscle
You can't inhale or exhale
You can't be left the fuck alone
You can't be joyous
You can't whistle Dixie
You can't leave your driveway
You can't shop at fancy stores
You can't be caught in certain neighborhoods
You can't drive an expensive car
You can't live in a white neighborhood
You can't live in a black neighborhood once whites move in
You can't take a flight of stairs

You can't ride your bike
You can't have a nervous breakdown
You can't get sick
You can't have asthma
You can't remind the police you're human
You can't be startled or show confusion
You can't be hard of hearing
You can't toss a football
You can't take a knee
You can't make a U-turn
You can't yield the right of way
You can't call the police
You can't sit handcuffed in a cop car
You can't show anger, sadness, emotion or rage
You can't yell out in pain
You can't point out what's absurd and insane
You can't fold yourself into origami and disappear
You can't even shut your eyes and pray
You can't just be left to your own devices
Like being black and breathing

Blue Dick Blue Balls

I just ate an egg
And tried to walk
On water but busted my ass
In the tub.

I'm not going to
Speculate. I
Don't have to, yo.
I exist in all time.

Past present future
All collide in my mind.
Ask my wife. Married her
Before we met. Regular riot.

Though I must admit, it's a
Little embarrassing. Me in this
Tub and all—flat on my ass. Oh,
God. Where's my watch, mane?

My enemies will pay
A price for vaping my
Blue-black Blackness,
Leaving me with no soap.

No squid pro quo for all the shit I did
For this damn planet. I'm not asking
For reparations. Just acknowledgment
And some drawers.

Hair! Hair!

I am seeking a certificate of live birth
For Donald Trumps' hair—

A red rooster sloshed and flopped
Over a sloped forehead's scrunched face;

A dead possum playing possum, propped-up
Roadkill on the windshield of his strained face—

I am checking for its authenticity
Does it exist in the same time zone

As his head which functions as a
Hollow silo for his receding brain

I am seeking the purity
Of each strand of hair in pain—

Waxed, dyed, fried, wrung
Like a wet mop and hung and slung

Every which way devil may care—
Hair! Hair!

It may be a distraction
It may espouse brash rash reactions

From the pie hole of his smug fat fish face,
Blow hard words caught in the gullet

Of a mouth never on pause, whose fabrications
And aspersions are claws stuck in the bottom

Of a barrel full of Dixie Land flags
Waving desperately in the wind of defeat

Like charred ash flakes from a
Bombed out lung

But I am also seeking the legitimacy
Of the hair on his tongue

Triptych

Old on a Greasy Urn

A POEM BY MELANIA TRUMP

To swat your husband like a fly
You must not tell a lie
Let him know how you feel
His hand is like a slimy seal
Slimier than his slimy heart
Smellier than his hollow fart
To swat your husband like a gnat
Irritated at his hair that looks like a cat
Sick of all his bullshit lies
Sicker of his long wide ties
When will he keel over on toilet like Elvis
When will he slip while tweeting and break pelvis
To swat your husband like a fly
To rebuke his every breathing lie
To get away from his agent orange flesh
In that dreadful White House mesh
All I wanted was to marry rich and be rich
Instead I'm stuck with this cruel bitch
Who just keeps bullshitting and tweeting
Only stopping for me to pee on him while he's bleating
Like a dumb sheep on all fours
As I run and slam White House doors
Yes the Lincoln bed will be cold tonight
And every night hereafter as we fight
I swat his hand and smack his face
And risk smearing orange on this vase

Trumpeo
No matter the temperature in my drawers,
I will not change them.

Climate change wants to keep
Poor white black lung disease white folks

Out of mines. Sure, come Christmas time they will find
Lumps of coal in their red hanging stockings. All I ever

Care about is besting the Black dude who held office
Before me. The elegant intelligent graceful one. Yeah,

I'm boorish. I'm whorish. I'm a Viking and Visigoth. I
Could care less about social graces. I could care less if

My thumbs are short and stubby and make women hurl.
Call me Earl. I'm not only the fisherman—I am the great white
    whale.

I open my mouth and eat all the blackness in the world.
What temperature is in my drawers? What temperment are my
    whores?

I work to blow smoke up the asses of white people too dumb and
    lazy to
Realize the lump they chew on their dinner plate ain't chuck beef
    but coal.

What I stole . . .
    From their hearts.

When Prostitutes Piss on Trump

When prostitutes piss on Trump
You can't tell the yellow from the fellow
You can't make out the agent from the orange
And when they start singing in heavy Russian
And his hair starts kicking up a can-can
His wet face smearing off its tan-tan
When prostitutes piss on Trump
And Puti tapes it all from beneath the bed
That strange squealing you hear
(Not no scene from *Deliverance*! No.)
Is Trump hogtied with his own tie
An apple sticking out his ass and mouth
The heat turned up in his Moscow motel sauna suite
The smell of pig skin and day-old bacon
Cooked in the rancid oil of a raggedy pan
And a pot to piss in overflowing with glisten
Trump so orange and pink and off-white
Hair matted to forehead and mattress
When prostitutes piss on Trump
In Russian as he sings "The Star-Spangled Banner"
His old dried out nuts all spent and tangled
Puti under the bed holding his breath
While Trump is screaming as the pee burns
A hole in the mattress so wide
He can see Sarah Palin looking like a deer
In headlights, slapping her knee, singing:
"Hambone, Hambone, have you heard ..."
Then, snatching off Trump's wet, musty, pissy-ass wig
With her mouth, squeaking like a church mouse:
"I can see Russia from my house!"

After Pelosi's Dropkick

Trump folded like a big beach chair.

Trump folded like a dirty dishrag.

Trump folded like his orange lace-front on the tarmac.

Trump folded like a Manchego cheese omelet.

Trump folded like a double chin hiding from Mitch McConnell in
a tortoise shell.

Trump folded like a dusty-ass dingy toupee batted away by a
pissed-off Pelosi.

Trump folded like a fat man's testicles caught in a George Forman
Grill.

Trump folded like a Japanese room divider.

Trump folded like a futon riddled with Ravioli stains, breadcrumbs
and beer farts.

Trump folded like Mitch McConnell's chin under a rolling pin.

Trump folded like a 35-day-old chorizo soft shell taco stampeded
by a caravan of petrified prayer
rugs at the Southern border.

Trump folded like Melania's eyelashes giving him the side-eye as
he hunches over her
in the Lincoln bed.

Trump folded like an enchilada at Denny's.

Pelosi crushed Trump like a beer can.

Pelosi sends Trump to his room to tweet, No fair, *Maaahhhhhm!!!*

Pelosi rode Trump around the White House lawn like a
hobby 🦄 horse.

Trump folded like his hair flap crouched underneath a Make
America Great Again hat.

Pelosi snatched Trump's wig.

Pelosi didn't even have to put Vaseline on her face and have
   someone hold her earrings to beat
      Trump's ass.
Trump folded like a parachute of snot and tears pouring out his
   fat-fish face after
      Pelosi told him—NO!!!
Trump folded like a plate of *hamberder* nachos.
Trump folded like a Spam sandwich.
Pelosi beat Trump like a dirty carpet.
Pelosi beat Trump with a stolen hotel bible.
Trump folded like orange cake batter.
Trump folded like Russian prostitute pee.
Trump folded like a Confederate flag in Southeast D.C.
Pelosi was Wu Tang Clan to Trump's Vanilla Ice.
Trump folded like the sweaty socks of defeat.
Trump folded like Bambú paper.
Pelosi broke her foot off in Trump's ass.
After Pelosi got through with Trump all he could do was spit out
   some teeth, look
      cockeyed and confused, swat aimlessly at stars, and mumble,
      Covfefe, Covfefe,
      Covfefe.
Trump folded like Mumbo Sauce on greazy-ass fries.
Covefefe is Russian for "To Cave."
Covefefe is Russian for Rosebud.
COVFEFE is Trump's anti-LGBTQ policy known as Don't Ask
   Can't Spell.
Pelosi beat Trump's ass like he stole the election.
Pelosi filleted Trump's ass and fried it in some fatback, Crisco Oil
   and vinegar.
Pelosi molly-whopped Trump with Aunt Esther's pocketbook.
Pelosi sent Trump's toupee running for the border.

Pelosi swatted Trump like a fruit fly.

Pelosi popped Trump like a pimple.

Trump folded like Rudy Giuliani's last strand of hair.

Trump folded like a Graham Cracker dunked in Milk of Magnesia.

Pelosi beat Trump like a dusty carpetbagger.

Pelosi rolled Trump like a freight train hobo.

Pelosi rolled Trump like tumbleweed.

Pelosi rolled Trump like a loose joint.

Pelosi gutted Trump like a Philly blunt.

Pelosi bumrushed Trump like KRS-1 did PM Dawn.

Trump folded like a Pamper stuffed in a Diaper Genie 😊 😊 😊

Pelosi ate Trump's liver with some fava beans and a nice Chianti.

Trump folded like an empty fortune cookie. 😩

Pelosi laced up her Timbs and STOMPED Trump's off-white ass
   into the White House lawn
     until a wall formed around his toupee.

TRUMP CONSIDERS US THE ENEMY.
   WE CONSIDER HIM THE ENEMA.

SHIT JUST GOT REAL.

Pelosi made Trump get the switch from the tree to beat his ass
   with.

Pelosi was Cardi B to Trump's Taylor Swift

Said little bitch, you can't fuck with me / If you wanted to

These expensive, these is red bottoms / These is bloody shoes!

Quincy Jones

Quincy Jones: Yeah, Michael (Jackson)
Used to dress like the Pope and babysit
The Boys from Brazil.
Interviewer: 👀 👀
Quincy Jones: You want that olive?
[Grabs it out of the martini tumbler.]
Thanks, bro. Love these shits.

Interviewer: . . . you were saying something
About Michael Jackson. . . ?

Quincy Jones: Man, these motherfuckin' crackers
Got this world all fucked up. Motherfuckers are
Vampires—straight up suck the blood out your ass
From the coffin!

Interviewer: 👀 👀 👀 👀

Quincy Jones: Yeah, man. Brando fucked a rhinoceros
In the Cincinnati Zoo. Rhino was on rollerblades.
What's that cologne you rockin'? Versace?
Yeah, I knew that motherfucker. Creepy.
Good teeth, though!

Interviewer: 👀 👀 👀 👀 👀 👀 👀 👀

Ghostwriting Meek Mill Dissing Drake

I just wanna know
If marbles help you
Pronounce words
Correck

I just wanna know
How many gold teefuses
It take to chew
A Snickers bar

I just wanna know
Was that a Snickers
Bar—or Cecil the Lion's
Last Will & Testicle

I just wanna know
If 1 & 1 make 2

I just wanna know
'Cause counting
Was never my
Strong suit

Matter of fack
You ain't wants no part
Of my Hannibal Lecter
White suit—

Lucky I rhyme wit' this
Face mask, too—
Woulda done bit
Your taco meat tiddy

Spit it out like
Mase & P-Diddy
Like that 5 million
Ganked from Fiddy

I just wanna know
What the fux I'm
Talkin' 'bout

Sometimes my rhymes
Just wander about
Like Thelonious Monk
On stage dancing in a circle

I just wanna know
Why the sky is blue

I just wanna know
If you is To Wong Foo

I just wanna know
If your moms remember
Me—and why
She wanted to name you
FiFi

I just wanna know
Why your rhymes
Got Lyme Disease

Was that *Versace Versace*
Versace or a donkey sneeze

I just wanna know
If that vice grip head
Was squeezed to make
Lemon Jello—

Hello?

How It Will Finally Come to an End

Trump on the toilet like Elvis
    Mainlining dry beef burgers
& hydroxychloroquine.
    Melania in the Lincoln bed-
Room dousing it with Lysol
    & Clorox to mask the smell
Emanating from the bathroom.

    An alarm is tripped. Secret Service
Can be heard managing muffled
    Screams as if kneed in the nuts.
A sniper on the roof can be heard
    Yelling as he falls into a burning
Bush. Protesters have breached the
    White White House fence. 🔥 Flames

Are everywhere. Trump doesn't even
    Have time to wipe his ass or send up
One last tweet before he falls on his
    Bloated face with a turd the size of a
1973 Buick sticking out his ass. Melania
    Rushes in with a PPE mask & is suddenly
Overcome by her husband's obnoxious

    Fumes. She can only manage a "Be best"
Between coughs. Trump is yelling to her
    To help him get the Lincoln log out
Of his ass as his face orange smears

The cold white tiles. As Melania struggles
With the turd cemented in her Doonky's
   Ass, protesters have lit the white White

House on fire. It resembles a tulip of flames.
   Melania finally comes to her senses & drags
Trump by the turd & his lace-front. She
   Manages to drag his fat ass down the stairs
But is met by elves donning MAGA hats singing,
   Oh oh, Antifa, we could make it together...
Melania, watching shit go up in flames, weighs
   Her options, grabs a few furs, her jewelry &
Trump's credit cards & leaves him to be
   Turned into a hobby horse for the MAGA elves.
She chunks up the deuces to Trump crying
   & blubbering like a bloated baby & says,
Be best! & bounces with the last & loneliest
   Secret Service agent left standing.

Well, You Needn't

Since vinyl is making a comeback
Along with fur slides, Snuffleupagus
Eyelashes and Cousin It weaves,
I must confess, this toxic masculinity's

Getting on my last recorded nerve.
Mofo's gotta come correck, as my
Auntie used to say. I'm often
Offended by these tone-deaf aggressive-

Ass superheroes with their disappearing
Acts, jumping out windows, hanging
Off fire escapes well after midnight
When my old man didn't even come—

Nor did I, which is the goddamn point.
But I'm not one to gossip, 'cause I'm
A lady. But this whole notion of coming
And going when you good and well please

Is really wearing out its welcome—
And my one good nerve. I'm not with that
Ditzy Lois Lane shit, I'll cut a motherfucker,
Cobwebs, cape, red boots, and all. Shoot,

My mama didn't raise no fool. I know when
A mofo is not truly interested in me
But for one thing. Hell, I'm stressed but
I'm damn sure no damsel in distress.

Yet I must confess—that I carries a
Razor blade between my cheek and gum
Like the chewing tobacco my grand-
Daddy used to dip and snuff. And I

Knows how to use it. So if you don't
Wanna lose it—or me for that matter—
Stay away from the motherfucking
Window.

TONY MEDINA

I Am the Churro Lady

I'm a nasty woman a bad hombre
Where once I used butacas to shake like maracas
And bash over the heads of gringo colonial cucarachas
I haven't softened over the years my heroics
Consist of cocinas and taco trucks I gives a fucks
About my chimichanga mofongo salchicha morcilla
Alcapurria—and yes, bitch, my churros that will
Give you churras if you say, *Don't drink the water!*
To be heroic to walk on water to escape las gangas
To dance with coyotes while desert sun beats me into
Heated sands quick to cross lands where my
Abuelita breastfed me while milking a skinny cow
Only to find myself reclaiming lands stolen from my
Great great great grans my abuelos and tíos and
Papás—to have my children die in pigeon coops
And pig pens while La Migra violates their brown Indio skins
Mira, hijo de puta, don't ever put your gringo claws
On my babies I will beat you down with my big-ass burritos
And hot cinnamon churros and scald you with the pan
Ay sangano déjame quieto déjame vivir
Mi vida do I need to speaky English?
Does my twirling tongue baffle you, baboso!
Fuck your pinche-piojo gardens and nasty toilets—
Wash your own damn platos y calzoncillos nobody wants to touch
Your dirty drawers anyway, sucio—you lazy pale pestilence
On an earth you carve up and scarf down like pizza—or my
    freaking churros
And now you wanna come for my tacos won't let me sell
My churros won't let me cross back into the land

Of the Indios my ancestors who built this country
Up con Africanos plucking poisoned grapes lavando platos
Wiping old viejo culos in nursing homes you dump your abuelos in
I am the Churro Lady I'm a nasty woman a bad hombre
Coming to brighten your world with my brown culo and black ass
Get used to it, estúpido! Coming to you in stereotypes in
Living color with my roach killers and Zoot suits with my
Souped-up lowrider taco trucks with my pañuelo and pots
And pans with a great big Dollar Store stolen spatula
To smack that pale ass—jupa de pollo
Conquistadores siempre da'me dolores ay, Papá Dios—ayúdame!
You picked the wrong motherflowers to cage
Get used to it, pendejo. I'm bringing my wet back and sand like
    hurricane
Humiliation and horrendous (h)oh-rree-bleh juevos get used to it,
    green-go
DNA is on my side like it's always been, coño—ya es tiempo,
    hombre
We don't need no stinking badges—canto cabrón—your time is up!

Five Chanclas of Death

Grandma used her chanclas like nunchucks. She had a hair on her chinny chin chin that coiled and stretched on command. If you ever sucked your teeth under your breath, huffing and puffing a side-eye, she'd whirl and whip it on you like the switch from a tree and light your ass up as you tried to make it out the door. She wore a bata all the time and everywhere like a second skin, with pockets that could hold *The New Gideon's Bible*, a rolling pin the size of a Louisville baseball bat, the *National Enquirer*, Bambú paper, a *TV Guide,* a remote control replete with corroded Double A battery acid crusted over the buttons, day-old Italian bread for the dirty pigeons she pinged unwittingly outside our window during feeding time, a paperback copy of Erica Jong's *Fear of Flying,* and an extra pair of brown chanclas smuggled from a Woolworth's on Fordham Road in the Boogie Down Bronx the summer the city had a garbage strike and the Son of Sam was running around like a sweaty dumpy Cyclops clod sneak-killing unsuspecting pedestrians and terrorizing New York City something fierce. If she had any more room in her pocket, she'd easily hoard sardine cans, Goya beans and Spam. No one ever asked her—and I don't know where the hell this came from—about her 8 1/2 x 11 inch framed newspaper cutout of Soupy Sales. One particular sticky night in the swampy South Bronx heat, just before the eleven o' clock news ended and *The Honeymooners* began, Grandma bounded down the rickety stairs of our Hunts Point five-floor walk-up in her worn-out chanclas and loose flowing tarpaulin-like bata heading for the subway with the determination of a pissed-off Pamplona bull. Alarmed, I shouted, *Grandma! Grandma! A dónde vas?* She shrugged me off and snapped, *Déjame!* When her chin hair started stretching and forming into a bastón—a rigid walking cane—holding up her Last of the Big Mamas weight, I knew where she was heading, but I left the crib without my asthma pump and all I could do between folding over like a table napkin trying to catch my breath saddled by my desperate intermittent wheezes was to manage to squeeze out another, *But, Grandma! No!* Without turning around, and flailing her floppy brown arms in the thick air, Grandma shouted back at me and a couple of winos huddle-praying to Jesus over some Muscatel in a back alley, *Carajo! Hijo de Uncle Sam! I'm going to get that pinche cabrón sin vergüenza if it's the last thing I do!* For some freaking reason, and perhaps the heat brings out the freaks, a good number of criminals were on the make at the unfortunate time that Grandma charged into the subway bellowing, *Dónde estás? Dónde estás?* Her chin hair churned sensing the motion of criminal behavior. Her chinny chin chin senses settled on a motofreaky hunched over a nasty splintered subway bench with the words BIATCH and DONDI LIVES graffitied on it. The graffiti rose up off the bench like a mummy trying to grab at Grandma. But with lightning speed she beat it back with a chancla that came out of nowhere. Without skipping a beat or forgetting the horny Humpty Dumpty hunched over the bench, she maneuvered her triggered chin hair like a Taser, giving the vulgar pendejo a little jolt. Grandma called him a philistine. He jumped up crying, *Ay chihuahua!* As the startled girl ran off, Grandma lengthened her thickening chin hair, hurling it back and whipping the chump in rapid succession—*Whoo Ta-chich! Whoo Ta-chich!*—followed by his—*Ay Ay-Ay! Ay Ay-Ay!*—clutching at his stinging glutes. Before he could make it up the stairs, Grandma reached into her pocket with the entire hoarder's catalogue clusterfuck and log-jammed with so much junk. Cramming her hand through the clunky morass, Grandma managed, without looking mind you, to produce a brand spanking new chancla with the price tag still dangling off it. As if a knife thrower, Grandma dinged the would-be rapist in the back of the head, paralyzing him as he dizzily waved at stars twirling just above his head. His drunk cockeyed self could not make heads or tails of the knot forming on his forehead like a woody. Grandma turned to me pointing with her lips—*Mira! Cheech and Chong*—at another suspect dude nodding into a serious Weeble Wobble lean-to, his face nearly scraping the gum-spackled platform, miraculously never touching the grimy ground. But then his stomach rumbled so loud we thought it was the downtown 6 train roaring into the station like a tornado or the Tasmanian Devil. It turned out to be a volcano of churras formulating like dark brown lava from his dingy-ass white Polyester pants from Easters gone by. *Ay fo!* Grandma yelled, her chin hair twitching and turning at the sudden choking fumes. The weight and violent heat and pestilence of the churras caused the tecato to tilt, jerk and tumble over the platform heading for the tracks to a deeper Dante's hell down below. As rats the size of polo ponies scrambled off, his dripping candle wax face torpedoed its way toward the train tracks. But before his forehead, nose and chin smacked into the third rail, Grandma knocked off two fat hobby horse rats with one boomeranging chancla hurl while her chin hair sprang out like a lightning cable, snapping its tentacle around his neck and yanking him up and out with such ferocity he didn't know what hit him. Grandma plopped Cheech and Chong onto a bench as his comatose high never skipped a beat, save for when he managed to lift his head and open his eyes to mumble through heroin drool, *Hey, man . . .* before he continued his deep space nod. Grandma turned to me, five vomit green Lee Press-On nails clutched at a holstered, battered brown chancla, and said, *Mi'jo, promise me you'll never end up like this.* She produced a fatty from the pocket of her bottomless bata and asked if I wanted to hit the blunt she was choking on. *Nah, Grandma. I'm good.* We climbed up out of the subway toward the sun's light. Grandma limped on one chancla salvaged from the six she rolled out the crib with. The newsstand had fresh copies of the *Daily News* with that hijo de puta Son of Sam's can of Spam face on the cover with the headline: CAPTURED. Grandma shouted at the man at the newsstand as if he had anything to do with the headlines, *Oye! It should begin with* CABRÓN, *cabrón!*

Yemayá

She dared resist the sun
     Thus turned herself into cloud
Overwhelmed & startled by
The sum & strength of her power
     Her quicksilver persistence
She cried & cried, nothing
Loud, released from hunched
     Shoulders a downpour
Of pain she renamed
Rain—*Oh, let it go*
     Let it go, the wind proclaimed
As life persisted &
In the rivers & oceans & seal-slick streets
     Down below

This Bullet Has My Blood

This bullet has my blood
    On its lips

This bullet chewed
    Through my shirt

& spit back
    Pink red brown flesh

This bullet choked on its
    Own dull gray powdered mesh

Sprinkled on my chest
            Like black pepper
On a chicken breast

This bullet choked & gasped
    & collapsed onto slick

Rain-drenched asphalt street
    Where my blood pools around

My heart crawling like red
    Army ants toward my feet

Kajieme Powell

He took 2 energy drinks
And some donuts
From a corner store
Placed them along the curb
Waiting for the cops to come
He paced back and forth
Anger and frustration
Stalking his undaunted thoughts
He wasn't gonna take it
Anymore—

The cops climbed the curb
With their patrol car
Drawing their semi-automatic guns
Right hand in his jacket pocket
Clutching a steak knife
He ordered them to *Kill me*
Kill me, Kill me now!
They lit him up
With 9 rounds
Till blood and smoke
Seeped from his flesh

They rolled him over like a log
His body's punctured skin
Pouting like lips
It took all 23 seconds
For his 25 years
To leak out his bleeding lungs

When the coroner got him
He asked the officers
To take the handcuffs off

This Is a Night for the Smiling Silence of Stars

Lightning bugs flickering in mason jars
Streetlight dancing on the brown yellow orange
    Tongue of November leaves batting like lashes
    In an Indian summer breeze

This is a night for the guiding light of polestars
And cars that hum through the arteries of the street
    Below a blue canopy lit with mason jars
A galaxy so vast yet discrete hangs like sheets
In wind soft as gauze

This is a night to occupy the palm of a hand
    Its double resting on the small of a back
Waltzing through the silent prayer of breathing

Death, With Occasional Smiling

The heart is a trampoline
    Everyone gets their kicks

   The gyre twists & turns
     Battening down the hatches

Death brings us to our knees
     Sand & time sift & tick

     The clucking you hear is far & near
Wind rakes us in its breeze

     We look up to find what light there's left
Makes shadows of our flesh

     Held together in a cathedral of bones
Arrogant architecture some grand design

     Decaying each hour diminishing
Like sunlight slanting through blinds

     Death smiling with lips of castanets

Simpson Street September

Sunlight pours in the
    Room grandma by the window
        Praying through black beads

I pretend I'm asleep
    Living in my own daydream
        Escaping the streets

I'm warm all over
    Heat covers me like a quilt
        Life is a kitchen

Full of sounds and smells
    With me under the table
        While grandma's cooking

Lifts me till I float
    Above broken-down buildings
        And flat fluffy clouds

On wings of prayer
    And humming
Garbage truck sounds

I Spoke to a Belgian Waffle Once

So you have radishes for teeth grinning frantically beneath
Hard-boiled eyes—*Surprise surprise*—this is what it means
To recklessly side-eye like a head-on collision of headlights
Cranked up high—*O the pressure the pressure*—of blood boiling
Over easy greasy a cop's approaching keep your hands in view
Grip the steering wheel till your knuckles turn white—*Yuck*
Yuck yuck—that's a joke homes we know you have butterfingers

Stabbing out each hand melting in the light cutting the night
Stalking your every breath we know that patrol car snuck up
On you when you least expected it lost in a blues so blue
It was black as the nightstick smearing with artificial light
Smudging fear with tears wiped across the windshield
Smack dab in the middle of forehead blood glass grinning
Teeth on lap pooling you apart—*O those snaggletooth radishes*

Stephon Clark

There are wrongs which even
the grave does not bury.
HARRIET ANN JACOBS

There'll be time enough
For blood blooming
Petals peeled
From overfed
      Flesh

A late night
Stroll, patrolling
The petunias in
Grandma's garden

No need for patio's
Light haloed by
Flies, spider webs
And moths flailing
Away as if drowning

In midair

      Oh who
Could tell in all
That dark, grass
Shifting beneath
Flat feet

Who
Could tell

The silhouette
In the dark
    Framed by
Starlight and distant
Windows
    Who
Could tell a body
From a target
Study at night

There'll be time enough
For blood blooming
Petals pierced
With lead-fed
    Flesh

The sin in the
Garden of breathing
Of being
    Black in
All that black

What falls is not
    Paradise
But twelve
Bullet shells
    The rest
Buried in the back

Dislodged out the chest

Blooming petals
Of blood
In the garden
In the garden
Of no more
Breathing
Of blackness

Leaving

The Great Pretender

I only pretend to be dead—death is a
Dress rehearsal for a show never to be played again
Dying is so easy like a dog rolling over,
Playing dead; I only pretend to bleed
These wounds don't need to heal
Something will bloom sooner or later

> *Oh, yes, I'm the great pretender*
> *Pretending I'm doing well*

This blood you see, what pools at
Your feet, don't mean much no more
What spreads and rises and stains
Your hands and feet—
The Nile *(Denial? Duh-dum duh-dum—Oh, hell!)*
I only pretend to be dead
This heart I have can play dead, too
Like a dog you teach a trick or two

> *Oh, yes, I'm the great pretender*
> *Pretending I'm doing well*

I only pretend to scream—don't you know?
These words I write, these words I scream
And curse—figments of the imagination
For those who have no imagination
Or if they do—
Spooks them white

Oh, yes, I'm the great pretender
Pretending I'm doing well

I only pretend to breathe; the movement
Of my lungs a mere optical illusion
You'll see soon enough
The air leaking out like a tire
Oh no—I'll never retire from playing dead
I'll never turn you down

Oh, yes, I'm the great pretender
Pretending I'm doing well
My need is such I pretend too much

God Awful Ghazal

No, I did not call the cops on white people for blinking.
No, I did not call the cops on white people for thinking.
No, I did not call the cops on white people for stinking.
No, I did not call the cops on white people for sinking.
No, I did not call the cops on white people for inking.
No, I did not call the cops on white people for linking
Up with other white people to do me harm, making me buy the farm.
No, I did not call the cops on white people for thinking
I'm something less than human and treating me as such.
No, I did not call the cops on white people for burning a cross
On the front lawn of my mind in order to terrorize the Holy Ghost
Out of me, and have me rethink religion.
No, I did not call the cops on white people for trying to erase me.
No, I did not call the cops on white people for ignoring my breathing.
No, I did not call the cops on white people for pronouncing my
     name wrong.
No, I did not call the cops on white people for fucking up a song.
No, I did not call the cops on white people for waylaying an assault
     on rhythm.
No, I did not call the cops on white people for culture jacking my
     memories.
No, I did not call the cops on white people for gentrifying my sense
     of self and self-
     esteem.
No, I did not call the cops on white people for displacing me from
     my dreams.
No, I did not call the cops on white people for eating my food,
     drinking my drink, warming

themselves by the fire I built, then ransacking my reality like
Visigoths.
No, I did not call the cops on white people for the kidnap and the
rape, for the torture, the lynch
   mobs, the fire hoses and barking biting dogs.
No, I did not call the cops on white people for disregarding my
humanity and my intelligence
   and the fact that I am a sentient being on the planet long before
they walked upright and
   attempted to wipe their asses.
No, I did not call the cops on white people because the cops, for
the most part, are white and
   white tends to only recognize white in the grand hard-on of
American reality, and more than
   likely would have turned on me, beating and brutalizing and
killing my ass like a racial
   memory reflex, turning me into a percussion instrument or a
human sprinkler system bleeding
   on the front lawn of American racism.

Running the Voodoo Down

I

Shango's red black raging mouth
H(O)wling Whys & Y's & Wise
Through headlight Djeli eyes
Lighting the way to
How we See & Sound

Scream & Shout
Who Who—WHOWHOWHO
Dat in

Coltrane's blazing horn
Smacking & scorching wooden Negroes
All Ascot no Fitzgerald
Cursing capitalists & the ghastly ghostly (g)utter
Audacity of their soul-sucking life-crushing corporations
Passing for people

II

O, you must've did something terrrrrribly right
Enough to be considered a one-man Axis of Evil
On the strength of one poem—a throwback broadside circa 1967,
    NewArk Rebellion
But we all know whowho whowho who the real "Axholes of Evil"
    is, as you put it
Who whowhowho who the pothead calling the kettle a crackhead O

III

Sheeeet! I could hear the barbershop & the corner now

That you—like Brenda Conner Bey & Louis Reyes Rivera & Jayne
Cortez & Tato Laviera & Wanda Coleman & John Watusi
Branch & Alvin Aubert & Malcolm's Griot, Jan Carew—now
Split—to be in that number with that Ancestral Spirit Rising
role call Big Band that always got Our back—Running the
Voodoo Down
For us forever

You the Poet Laureate of the Out & Way Out now w/ I&I Bob,
man & Larry's hoodoo hollerin Bebop ghost —Black Boogaloo
Wailers wailing atop the Great Night Whale Hey, man. You
split?

On your way out you smacked the shit out of Kanye w/ a
Confederate flag—didn't you?

I could hear the bloods on the block now on the corner in the
barrios & bodegas—
"Mira, Amiri se fue!!!"
In barbershops & hair salons in bars on prison yards—*Whoooooooooo*

BARAKA SO BAD HE TOOK SHARON WITH HIM!!!

Damn near made McGreavy & O'Reilly shit they drawers

Creepy-ass crackers hiding in them Bushes with Rummy Wolfy
Condi Colon

& that Constipated corpse Cheney

Killed more Palestinians & Iraqis w/ Ariel raids than all the black
poems

Ever spoke—or written!

What anti do dat qualify as, Motherflower?

IV
[Dis da Intermission]

Pass me a copy of the *New York Times*
So I could wipe my ass

V
Critics are bullshit
Unless they are lemmings
Plopped on a stair
Master stair(ing)
Way (up) to Heaben

VI
Let us not confuse controversy with clarity
The lies of incongruous whores with integrity

VII
Baraka spoke in a language of Bopulicitous intent
James Brown black Langton Hughes blue
Mouth of Malcolm Baldwin eyes
Big as suns & moons
Making sure we never in the dark—
With ghosts!

VIII
Imamu spoke in a language
Unshakable sylla-stanza-break-dance-able funk lore free

Yet always with that tenderness & slant he peeped in Miles
Full of a lyrical expanse that climbed its rhythm
Deep into the cathedral of your bones

Amiri spoke in a language
Robeson rich DuBois direct Left a Hughes impression
With him *Ooom Boom ba Boom* Tubman-Turner tongue
Our fighter pilot literary Ali each poem a butterfly stick & move
    sting
Some mowed down like bowling pins some machine gunned to a
    certain degree

One hand on the boulder of the struggle, the other
Clutching a javelin—dagger balanced on tongue—
Spoke in Griot-Speak like Sisyphus Speak(s)—

> *Your hair could go white*
> *As mine you roll a boulder*

> *Uphill as many times I have*
> *In my life*

> *Hair can go white*
> *Curse enough ghosts as I have*

> *Hair whiter than John Brown's bones*

IX

The day before my birthday the phone rang off the hook.
Part of me shut out the words. The other half refused to take a
    knee.
Part of me needed to be numb to the feeling, what was

Reeling, inside of me, a fish line taking off at the hook.

The day before my birthday the phone rang off the hook.
Part of me was shook. Two walls closed in on me, as I
Gripped the phone and clenched my teeth, and felt a
Shift in the room. I reached for the bourbon I kept
For a different occasion, and played all I had

Of Trane and imagined you reversing course,
Galloping out his horn, punching holes through
Death's neon smoky air. Outside rain splintered
Into kisses, winds bickered and brushed branches across

The window, blessing the house with confusion.
Inside more horses jumped up out of horns, a crush
Of black angels swirled, while Kentucky bourbon
Strummed me along. Somewhere I heard a bomb

Dropping. Somewhere I heard a baby screaming.
Somewhere a world was careening, and poets were
Dreaming, you'll come home, you'll come home.
Transition strained above my head and Trane

Burned through me with a murderous rage, and from deep
Within those flames, I succumbed to a certain sadness
And gravity of hurt that had been growing heavier as
Day slumped into night and the night receded into the
Small hours, until I felt a buzzing whisper in my ear,
And heard you sing:

When I die, the consciousness I carry I will to
Black people. May they pick me apart and take the

Useful parts, the sweet meat of my feelings. And leave
The bitter bullshit rotten white parts
Alone.

X

Great Spirits do not die.
They are forces
Of nature—
Energy forever
Passing through our
Souls, agitating
Our bones to
MOVE

XI

When the Teacher Speaks the Student Listens

Now
More than
Ever

At Copeland's

A cigarette dangles from your mouth
Like a flag at half-staff, the
Brim of a black felt hat held
Close, clutched in fingers' sweaty
Grip, above the open-mouth wail
Of a hungry grave. Ashes to
Ashes, dust to dust. A wooden box
Lowered into six feet of stone
Cold throat. Death's esophagus
Waits patiently for box & bone
Like holy communion, like a dog
Bored with what's in its pail.
Knows no prayer could interrupt
The hands lowering such precious cargo
Into the dank dusty lair. Knows
The fill & hull of this ship could
Not reverse its course from prayer's
Passage. A limp avalanche of ash
Makes its way through the soil tossed
On the flat blank face of
Coffin's indifferent stare. Somewhere
In there, something is screaming.

In Venice Dolphins Swim the Canals

As L.A. skies are crystal ball clear
Predicting the coming of the cicadas
& DC's cherry blossoms opening early
Like parasol debutante umbrellas

The streets are empty everyone is
Sheltered in as a virus rages like Ralph
Ellison invisible to the naked eye
While a naked ape an orange idiot

Sans the savant is babbling about
It being a hoax a hoax *it's all a hoax*
Telling us from the white White House
Don't believe your lying eyes as

Refrigerated trucks in Brooklyn
Stockpile bodies in freezers like popsicles
This agent orange menace is a virus
Unto himself as racism is as stupidity is

In a country where Confederate statues
Are more visible than common sense
A virus named after a cheap piss water beer
This menace barks *Chi-na Chi-na Chi-na*

As if repulsed by his wife's va-gi-na
At a press conference he bogarts the mic
From the experts who know more about
Science than he knows about stealing

Telling us hydroxychloroquine malaria
Pills are good as Tic Tacs at fighting
Bad breath—he should know—and if that
Doesn't work you could spray down

Your tongue with Lysol or belt back
Some Clorox to crank your box
In Venice dolphins swim the canals free
Of debris while here black joggers are hunted by

Fathers and sons in a rite of passage
Jim Crow outdoor trailer trash parlor game
As Amy or Karen or Becky with the bad brains
Scream hysterically into cellphones at 911 operators

In their worst Stanislavski Method acting
Like the black birder is a mockingbird
While an essential worker EMT cannot get
Any PPE instead she got 8 bullets into

Her bone-tired sleeping body in a 21-gun
Salute to T.S. Elliot with a side of side-eye
Because May is the cruelest month especially
During a lockdown where racism and hate

Are never quarantined yet a black man
Remains a stepping stool for a white man's
Knee who drummed out Colin Kaepernick
As if a flag takes precedence over a black life

NOTES

"Dame un Traguito" is for Tato Laviera, a major figure of the
    Nuyorican Poetry Movement.

"Father, Son Arrested in the Death of" is for Ahmaud Arbery, a
    25-year-old Black man, shot to death on February 23, 2020 while
    jogging by father and son, Gregory and Travis McMichael, in
    Brunswick, Georgia.

"Brother Can You Spare a Crime?" has italicized lines riffing off of
    Ernest Hemingway's short story "A Clean, Well-Lighted Place."

"Senryu for Trayvon Martin" is also for Joel Dias Porter (DJ
    Renegade). Trayvon Martin was a 16-year-old Black boy killed
    by George Zimmerman, a neighborhood volunteer security
    guard, who shot Trayvon Martin in a racial profiling incident at
    Trayvon's father's apartment complex in Sanford, Florida.

"Bert Williams" is for Bert Williams, an African American
    performing artist of the Vaudeville, Minstrel and Chitlin Circuit,
    considered to be the greatest American entertainer of his day.
    Williams, forced to perform in blackface, was a triple threat as
    dancer, singer and actor.

"Charleena Lyles" is for Charleena Lyles, a pregnant Black woman
    shot to death by two Seattle, Washington police officers in front
    of her three children after she called police for protection from
    her estranged boyfriend, reported as a burglary.

"From the Crushed Voice Box of Freddie Gray" is based on the
    death of Freddie Carlos Gray, Jr., a 25-year-old Baltimore,
    Maryland resident, following his brutal arrest and subsequent
    lapse into a coma.

"#IfIDieinPoliceCustody" relates incidents of police brutality where
    victims handcuffed behind their backs end up shot in their
    chests; and their deaths ruled suicides by medical examiners.

"A Few Small Nips" and "The Broken Column" are based on Frida
Kahlo's self-portraits, *A Few Small Nips* and *The Broken Column*.

"I Carry My Father's Name in My Name" is based on President
Barack Obama's estranged relationship with his Kenyan father
depicted in his memoir, *Dreams from My Father: A Story of Race
and Inheritance*.

"In the Window of the Cuchifrito Joint" derives from Cuchifrito
fast food restaurants in Puerto Rican neighborhoods.
Cuchifritos consist of pig intestines, pig's ears, fritters, and other
assorted delicacies.

"Antwon Rose" is for Antwon Rose II, a 17-year-old Black boy
fatally shot on June 19, 2018 by East Pittsburgh, Pennsylvania
police officer Michael Rosfeld.

"Two Eintou: Stevedore, Louisiana" is based on Russell Lee's
photograph, *Stevedore, Louisiana*.

"Bones in Tow" is based on Jamal Sullivan's painting, *Cliffs of
Hawaii*.

"Broke Campaign Contribution" and "Broke Lives Matter" are
persona poems from the perspective of a homeless everyman
named Broke.

"Two Days after Christmas" is for Toni Wells, a 22-year-old mother
murdered by her philandering husband, Barry Wells, who
choked and pushed her down a flight of stairs of their Brooklyn
brownstone apartment, December 27, 2017. Police were called by
Wells' neighbor but they neglected to leave their patrol car, let
alone knock on the door.

"Partial Transcript of Richie Incognegro's FOX Interview" satirizes
football player Richie Incognito who was accused of using the
N-word while hazing and harassing a Black teammate.

"After Pelosi's Dropkick" italicizes the nonword *hamberder* to
highlight the way Trump mistakenly spelled hamburger in a

tweet. Italicized ending lines are sampled from Cardi B's "Bodak
   Yellow" from *Invasion of Privacy* (Atlantic, 2018).

"Quincy Jones" is based on an interview of Quincy Jones in *Vulture*
   magazine.

"Ghostwriting Meek Mill Dissing Drake" is based on a Hip Hop
   beef between rap artists Meek Mill and Drake.

"Yemayá" is an African deity of the Yoruba tradition of Nigeria.
   Yemayá, regaled in yellow, is the powerful goddess of the ocean
   and of water.

"Kajieme Powell" recounts the last moments of 25-year-old
   Kajieme Powell, suffering from mental illness, who was shot
   to death by St. Louis police on August 19, 2014, ten days after
   Michael Brown's death in Fergusson, Missouri.

"This Is a Night for the Swirling Silence of Stars" is for Joanne and
   Alexander Gabbin.

"Simpson Street" pays homage to Simpson Street, a street in
   the South Bronx where I resided as a very young child before
   moving to other areas of the Bronx, New York.

"Stephon Clark" is based on the shooting death by Sacramento,
   California police of 22-year-old Stephon Clark on the evening
   of March 18, 2018 in his grandmother's backyard. The epigraph
   is from Harriet Ann Jacobs's *Incidents in the Life of a Slave Girl*
   (first published in 1861; reprinted by Penguin Classics in 2000).

"The Great Pretender" borrows its italicized lines from Buck Ram's
   song, "The Great Pretender," on The Platters' single *The Great
   Pretender* (Mercury Records, 1955).

"Running the Voodoo Down" was composed for Amiri Baraka's
   funeral held at Newark Symphony's Sarah Vaughn Hall in
   Newark, New Jersey. The title derives from Miles Davis'

"Miles Runs the Voodoo Down" from *Bitches Brew* (Columbia
   Record, 1970). In this poem, I sample lines (italicized in the last

stanza of part IX) from Amiri Baraka's poem, "LeRoy," from *Black Magic* (Bobbs-Merrill, 1969).

"Double Dare" concerns itself with the death of George Floyd, a 46-year-old Black man killed by Derek Chauvin, and two other Minneapolis, Minnesota police officers, on May 25, 2020. As Floyd was supine in the streets with his hands cuffed behind his back, Chauvin kneeled on his neck for 9 minutes as two officers held him down while the fourth yielded him from onlookers. Floyd was suffocated as he cried out for his mother and repeatedly uttered, "I can't breathe."

"In Venice Dolphins Swim the Canals" refers to the death of George Floyd (see above note) and the death of Breonna Taylor, a 26-year-old Black woman who was fatally shot in her Louisville, Ky., apartment on March 13, 2020, when white plainclothes officers Jonathan Mattingly, Brett Hankison, and Myles Cosgrove, executing a so-called "no-knock" warrant as part of a drug-related investigation, forced entry into her apartment and fired 32 rounds at Taylor and her boyfriend, Kenneth Walker. Taylor, an emergency room technician, was not a suspect in the investigation.

ACKNOWLEDGMENTS

Immense gratitude to the editors and publishers of the following anthologies and journals where versions of these poems first appeared, sometimes with different titles.

The A-Line: A Journal of Progressive Thought: "Still Life with Rick James Braids, Red Dream Book and Velvet Jesus"

About Place Journal: "One Guy Shot Another Guy," "Hair! Hair!" and "City of Floating Coffins"

African Voices: "Poem for Hugo Chávez" and "Dame un Traguito"

Beltway Poetry: "Deep Sea Blues," "At Copeland's" and "Oscar Peterson"

Gargoyle: "Stephon Clark," "Kajieme Powell," "Charleena Lyles" and "God Awful Ghazal"

LIPS: Thirty Fifth Anniversary Issue: "This Is a Night for the Smiling Silence of Stars"

North American Review: "Dame un Traguito"

Paterson Literary Review: "Holy Communion"

Saranac Review: "Bert Williams"

"Running the Voodoo Down" appears in the anthology *Brilliant Flame! Amiri Baraka: Poems, Plays, Politics for the People* (Third

World Press, 2018); "Dame un Traguito" appears in the anthology *¡Manteca!: An Anthology of Afro-Latin@ Poets* (Arte Público Press, 2018); "Hair! Hair!" and "I Spoke to a Belgian Waffle Once" appear in the anthology *Nasty Women & Bad Hombres: A Poetry Anthology* (Lascaux Editions, 2017); "Deep Sea Blues" appears in *Ocean Voices: An Anthology of Ocean Poems* (Spinner Publications, 2018); "Poem for Hugo Chávez" appears in *Poets Against the Killing Fields* (Trilingual Press, 2007); "From the Crushed Voice Box of Freddie Gray" and "Senryu for Trayvon Martin" appear in the anthology *Revisiting the Elegy in the Black Lives Matter Era* (Routledge, 2019); "From the Crushed Voice Box of Freddie Gray" and "#IfIDieinPoliceCustody" appear in the anthology *Resisting Arrest: Poems to Stretch the Sky* (Jacar Press, 2016); "Song without a Flag," "Dame un Traguito," and "Sunken Place Blues" appear in the anthology *Show Us Your Papers* (Main Street Rag, 2020); "Senryu for Trayvon Martin" appears in the anthology *Stand Our Ground: Poems for Trayvon Martin & Marissa Alexander* (FreedomSeed Press, 2013); "Antwon Rose," "Still Life with Rick James Braids," and "Red Dream Book and Velvet Jesus" appear in the anthology *400 Years: The Story of Black People in Poems Written From Love 1619–2019* (Broadside Lotus Press, 2019); "Banner day," "Blue Dick Blue Balls," "Five Chanclas of Death," "The Original" and "Well, You Needn't" appear in the anthology *The Future of Black: A Comics & Afrofuturism Poetry Anthology*, edited by Len Lawson, Cynthia Manick and Gary Jackson (Blair Press, 2021); "Father, Son Arrested in the Death of," "Double Dare," "Stephon Clark" and "In Venice the Dolphins Swim the Canals" appear in the anthology *Where We Stand: Poems of Black Resilience*, edited by Melanie Henderson, Enzo Silon Surin and Truth Thomas (Cherry Castle Publishing, 2021).

"Running the Voodoo Down" is a poem written for the occasion of Amiri Baraka's passing. It was read at his funeral service at the Sarah Vaughan Concert Hall, Newark Symphony Hall, on January 18, 2014. The poem was quoted in part in the *New York Times*.

Thanks to publisher Michael Broder, managing editor Samantha Pious, and book editor I.S. Jones at Indolent Books. Much love and thanks to Kimberly A. Collins, Rachel Eliza Griffiths, Cornelius Eady, Pamela Sneed, Sheree Renée Thomas, Alexa Muñoz, Patricia Biela, and Beverly Blackwell for their support in bringing this title to light. I would also like to thank my colleagues in the Department of English at Howard University for the freeing up of time toward the completion of this book.

ABOUT THE AUTHOR

TONY MEDINA is the author/editor of twenty-one books for adults and young readers, including *I and I, Bob Marley* (2009) and *The President Looks Like Me & Other Poems* (2013). Medina has received numerous accolades including the Paterson Prize for Books for Young People, a Langston Hughes Society Award, and the first African Voices Literary Award. His anthology, *Resisting Arrest: Poems to Stretch the Sky*, was published by Jacar Press in 2016. His debut graphic novel, *I Am Alfonso Jones*, received numerous honors including The New York Public Library Best Books for Teens, and was a Barnes and Noble bestseller. His book *Thirteen Ways of Looking at a Black Boy* received the Lee Bennett Hopkins Poetry Award and an Arnold Adoff Poetry Award Special Recognition. Medina has read/performed his work all over the United States, as well as in Puerto Rico, Germany, France, Poland, the Bahamas, and the Netherlands. He is the first professor of creative writing at Howard University.

ABOUT INDOLENT BOOKS

Indolent Books is a nonprofit poetry press based in Brooklyn. Indolent publishes innovative, provocative, and risky work by poets and writers who are queer, trans, nonbinary (or gender nonconforming), intersex, women (of all races and ethnicities), people of color (of all genders), people living with HIV, people with histories of addiction, abuse, and other traumatic experiences, and other poets and writers who are underrepresented or marginalized, or whose work has particular relevance to issues of racial, social, economic, and environmental justice. We also focus on poets over 50 without a first book. Indolent is committed to an inclusive workplace. Indolent Books is an imprint of Indolent Arts, a 501(c)(3) charity.

CPSIA information can be obtained
at www.ICGtesting.com
Printed in the USA
LVHW082049240222
711939LV00012B/493

9 781945 023262